A GIFT

FOR

FROM

DATE

Personal Notes
T O   T H E
GRADUATE

24 Values to Shape Your Destiny

LAURIE BETH JONES

COUNTRYMAN®

Nashville, Tennessee

Published by J. Countryman®, a division of Thomas Nelson, Inc., Nashville, Tennessee 37214

The King James Version of the Bible (KJV).

The New King James Version (NKJV) © 1979, 1980, 1982, 1992, Thomas Nelson, Inc., Publisher. Used by permission.

The Message (MSG) © 1993. Used by permission of NavPress Publishing Group.

New Century Version (NCV) © 1987, 1988, 1991, by Thomas Nelson, Inc. All rights reserved.

The *New Revised Standard Version of the Bible* (NRSV), © 1989 by the Division of Christian Education of the National Council of the Churches of Christ in the USA. Used by permission.

The Jerusalem Bible (TJB) © 1968 by Darton, Ongman, & Todd, Ltd., and Doubleday & Co., Inc. Used by permission.

The Contemporary English Version (CEV), © 1991 by The American Bible Society. Used by permission.

J. Countryman® is a trademark of Thomas Nelson, Inc.

Project Editor: Kathy Baker

Designed by Koechel Peterson & Associates | Minneapolis, MN

ISBN 1–4041–0304–X

Printed and bound in the United States of America

www.jcountryman.com | www.thomasnelson.com
www.lauriebethjones.com

Dear Graduate,

You have been granted and have earned many gifts through your dedication and commitment to education. By following through on a long and sometimes difficult process, you have proven that you can tackle a task and stay with it until your goals are reached.

As you embark upon your new life, you have a limitless horizon.

The light that will guide you on your journey will come from your family, your friends, your faith, and your community.

But perhaps the inner light that will serve you the most is the one based upon values. This book reflects my thoughts on values that will shape your soul and your destiny.

I hope you gain some new insights as you read these words, knowing that you were created by God for a high and holy purpose that only you can achieve.

Blessings to you,

Laurie Beth Jones

YOU HAVE
a limitless horizon.

FREEDOM

THERE ARE TWO KINDS OF FREEDOM IN THE WORLD: ONE IS FREEDOM THAT OTHERS GIVE YOU, AND THE OTHER IS THE FREEDOM YOU GIVE YOURSELF. IN A BOOK OF POETRY I WROTE YEARS AGO, I SHOWED A WOMAN'S HAT WITH A BIG FEATHER IN IT HANGING ALL ALONE ON A HAT RACK. I WROTE, "ANYONE CAN GIVE ME THE MONEY TO BUY HATS, BUT ONLY I CAN GIVE ME THE FREEDOM TO WEAR THEM."

Jesus spoke to a young man who had all the material wealth and freedom of his age. Yet Jesus looked into the man's soul and saw that he was not free—and could not be free until he gave up his bondage to material things (LUKE 18:22).

Jesus also observed a woman who had no visible financial freedom at all but who gave her very last dime to the offering plate. He marveled at how free her faith had made her on the inside (LUKE 21:2–4).

There was a movie recently called *The Hurricane* about an African–American boxer who was imprisoned for a crime he did not commit. Knowing he was innocent, one way he kept himself from becoming bitter was to daily reaffirm his mental freedom. He read avidly and bettered himself through knowledge. By freeing himself from ignorance and hatred on the inside, he prepared to be free on the outside when his conviction was overturned.

As a nation we stand for liberty. Hundreds of thousands of brave and loyal soldiers have died so that we could have the right to be free to determine our own destiny and to live lives of our own choosing.

Freedom of speech, freedom of the press, freedom to worship—all are rights that we take for granted daily.

We are blessed beyond measure to live in a nation that prizes external freedoms so highly.

Yet the freedom I want you to contemplate is the kind that is on the inside. Does your heart soar with hope and aspiration, or are you chaining yourself to past mistakes—errors of your own or those of your parents?

I believe God created each of us to be free—free to dream, and hope, and strive, and fail, and learn, and achieve.

A friend of mine once told me a saying that has stuck with me. She said, "I daily repeat to myself, 'I am where I choose to be.'" I have pondered those words many times.

That phrase takes away all victimhood and regret, and it places responsibility squarely on the shoulders that were meant to carry your freedom—your own.

Free to be you and me. Internally and externally, unto eternity. *Freedom.* What a glorious word. For the inside—and outside—of you.

'I AM WHERE I CHOOSE TO BE.'

RESPECT

I heard a saying recently: "If you would do well in the affairs of life, see the sacred in everything and everyone and leave the rest to God."

Sometimes we confuse respect with agreement, or even understanding. Chances are you may never fully understand the people around you. Odds are that you will not always agree with them either. Yet whether you agree or disagree, understand or are completely baffled by another's choices and behaviors, you can always give them respect.

When Mother Teresa was confronted with the hordes of dying people in India, she didn't seek to heal them all. She couldn't. She said, "I just wanted to show them respect before they died." Her desire to see the sacred in even the lowliest and neediest person led her to become a modern–day saint.

Scripture tells us to watch our behavior and to always show respect because "some have entertained angels unawares" (HEBREWS 13:2 KJV). Jesus also said, "Anything you did for even the least of my people here, you also did for me" (MATTHEW 25:40 NCV). In an amazing transfer of identity he was teaching us that showing respect to others is the same as showing respect to God.

When we try to get others to act like us, dress like us, think like us, and be like us, are we really loving them? Or are we trying to merely comfort our own egos with mirrored images?

It is perhaps as hard to respect ourselves as it is to respect other people. For some of us, it is easier to put others' feelings and needs and opinions ahead of our own.

Yet Jesus said we must love our neighbors as we love ourselves. The two types of love are intertwined.

God respects us so much that we are given immutable free will. We are allowed to choose life or death, heaven or hell, connection or separation, respect or disrespect.

Ultimately our choices come back to us.

One of God's favorite games is disguise.

It is therefore a sign of wisdom and intelligence to respect others, even strangers we don't understand. Respect is the key to the kingdom of knowledge, and peace, and love.

You can respect someone without loving them. But you can never love someone without showing them respect. Anyone who thinks or does otherwise is doubling back on their own path to heaven.

RESPECT

GOD RESPECTS US SO MUCH
that we are given immutable free will.

RESPECT IS THE KEY TO THE
KINGDOM OF KNOWLEDGE,
AND PEACE, AND LOVE.

ETHICS

ETHICS MEANS "THE STUDY OF
STANDARDS OF CONDUCT AND MORAL
JUDGMENT; MORAL PHILOSOPHY;
THE SYSTEM OR CODE OF MORALS
OF A PARTICULAR PERSON, RELIGION,
OR GROUP."

Ethics, ethos, and *ether* all come from the same root word, which relates to "atmosphere." Ethical behavior can never be independent from an ethical atmosphere. The corporate scandals of Enron, WorldCom, and other huge, publicly entrusted companies show that even good people can make poor choices when the atmosphere is poisoned.

Loose talking . . . loose thinking . . . blurry boundaries . . . a little fudging here and there led to economic disasters of unheard–of proportions. Individually, perhaps, the people who made poor choices might not have done so if the atmosphere in the companies had been different. If the talk was about service instead of profit, for example, decision makers would have had other people's images, rather than dollar bills, engraved on their hearts and minds.

Your actions ultimately will be determined by the "air" and "talk" you are breathing and speaking. Do not assume that your character alone can withstand impure talking and thinking. Many people stronger than you have failed.

Ethics and atmosphere are inseparable.

So where are you hanging out?

What "ethical" air are you breathing?

ETHICS AND ATMOSPHERE

ARE INSEPARABLE.

COURAGE

Some people confuse strength with courage. There is a difference.

Quite simply, strength is when you are able to break the rock.

Courage is when you are able to have the rock break on you.

When Rosa Parks ignited the civil rights movement because she refused to rise from her rightful seat on the bus, that was courage. When a Chinese student carrying a bag of groceries placed himself defiantly in front of the menacing tank in Tiananmen Square, that was courage. When Mikhail Gorbachev brought down the Communist Empire, declaring his own form of government to be unsustainable, that was courage.

When Jesus stood silent before his accusers, that was courage (MATTHEW 26:63).

When anyone stands up to the forces that would crush them and says, "Here I stand, and I can do nothing else," that is courage.

To be willing to give your life for a higher cause, that is courage.

People who show courage may hear whispering, or even shouting, in their ears, but somehow they allow courage—not fear—to have the last word.

What rock is hovering over you, challenging your courage?

Strength is when you are able to break the rock.

Courage is when you are able to have the rock break on you.

FRIENDSHIP

One of my favorite quotes about friendship says, "To have a friend is to live two lives." Through the eyes of our friends we see new things, experience the heights of joy and despair, and are blessed with different perspectives on how life can be lived. Friends take us beyond ourselves and also bring us back to our highest selves.

Friends bring us flowers when the world is tossing mud. Friends stay with us when everyone else has left the room. Friends huddle with us in the dark when we are frightened and run laughing through the field with us when we are full of joy. Friends often see the greatness in us that we refuse to see in ourselves. Friends are the face of God, the hand of God, the smile of God, the truth of God, the laughter of God, the comfort of God. Friends help us open the lemonade stand when the world has given us lemons, and friends are our first and best customers, telling all their other friends about us. Friends help us paint the signs over our careers and help us pack the boxes when we change them.

Friends see the good in us when everyone else has given up. Friends cry with us when our pets die and search high and low to help us find that perfect new puppy. A friend's slap on the back can clear our throats and snap our heads up to look at things differently. When we get so sick that our hair falls out, our friends shave their heads, too, and make a party out of it. When we stumble in the race and end up in a heap, our friends turn back and lift us up so we all cross the finish line together.

In our society we make much about the love of family, God, and country. Most of the songs we hear today on the radio have to do with romantic love. Yet in the Bible Jonathan entreated his friend David never to stop loving him (1 SAMUEL 20:42), and Ruth told Naomi, "Whither thou goest, I will go" (RUTH 1:16 KJV). Friendship, also, is to be highly prized.

Jesus said no one has greater love than to lay down his or her life for a friend (JOHN 15:13). He certainly proved his affection and regard for us as friends when he laid down his.

Choose your friends carefully. Apart from the books you read and the places you go, your friends will determine your destiny more than any other factor. Scripture says that anyone who finds a friend has found a true treasure (ECCLESIASTES 4:8–12). Treat your friends as the treasures they are, and you will be richer for it.

Friends

FRIENDS ARE THE FACE OF GOD,

THE HAND OF GOD, THE SMILE OF GOD,

THE TRUTH OF GOD, THE LAUGHTER

OF GOD, THE COMFORT OF GOD.

Apart from the books you read
and the places you go,
your friends will determine your destiny
more than any other factor.

HUMILITY

HUMILITY IS THE CHARACTERISTIC THAT MOST EXCITES THE FAVOR OF GOD. JESUS SAID, "ALL WHO EXALT THEMSELVES WILL BE HUMBLED, AND THOSE WHO HUMBLE THEM-SELVES WILL BE EXALTED" (LUKE 14:11 NRSV). HE ALSO SAID, "BLESSED ARE THE MEEK, FOR THEY SHALL INHERIT THE EARTH" (MATTHEW 5:5 NKJV). BEING A STUDENT OF LEADERSHIP HAS ALLOWED ME TO STUDY THE CHARACTER TRAITS THAT WILL MOST OFTEN CAUSE A PERSON TO MAKE A POSITIVE DIFFERENCE IN THE WORLD.

Although history is full of the names of conquerors and conquistadors, queens and rulers, explorers and people who somehow had access to those who make monuments, heaven's history book is going to be full of names that you and I have never before heard. Jesus said that anyone who even stops to give someone a drink of water will not have the deed go unnoticed (MATTHEW 25:40). God knows all the good that is being done in the world, and odds are that most of it is not being seen or discussed.

Jesus was the most humble man who ever walked the face of the earth, yet he never spoke ill of himself. I think that often we mistake humility with low self–esteem, and that is an error in judgment. Humility means knowing your rightful place both in the world and also in heaven. It means knowing that you are no better or worse than the lowest person on earth, and yet you're invited to a heavenly banquet that will last through eternity. It means knowing your gifts and recognizing that while you are not the source of those gifts, you have a responsibility to use them wisely for the good of all.

Humility means that because you were born with nothing and will die with nothing, you have nothing in this world to brag about or be attached to or consider your own.

Humility means understanding that what you see in the mirror is only a temporary form, as is whatever is in your bank account, your portfolio, or your safety deposit box.

Humility is recognizing that there is a Force greater than your own, and a Love greater than any you can imagine.

Humility will not rush to accept the award, but will hurry to wash the feet of those who got there late because of burdens too heavy to carry on their own.

When people enter the cave that many historians now believe is the birthplace of Christ, the opening is so small that all but children have to stoop to enter. Pilgrims have to bow as they approach him.

When one recognizes that the grains of sand by the sea are as numerous as the stars in the sky, that is humility. Humility neither shouts nor boasts, begs nor whines. Humility listens and is silent before the face of God.

HUMILITY MEANS KNOWING YOUR
RIGHTFUL PLACE BOTH IN THE
WORLD AND ALSO IN HEAVEN.

FAITH

Faith is the essence of things hoped for, the evidence of things not seen (HEBREWS 11:1). Faith has long been described as a spiritual necessity—an ingredient in religious life that one must have in order to be in relationship with God. Yet the physical aspects of faith also have been explored in recent years, particularly in association with advances in quantum physics. How does faith work, and why?

I believe one of our highest callings on earth is to be co-creators with God—to use our imagination, talents, dreams, and ideas to help bring about heaven on earth. Doing so means that we must have a clear picture of the desired end result. When Jesus pointed out that if you ask your Father for bread, he isn't going to send you a stone (LUKE 11:11), he was not only talking about the importance of asking but of being specific in our requests.

So faith at one level means being clear about what we want to see happen and then being specific about our request.

Once we have prayed our request to God, then we must do three things. The first is to release our request to God, knowing that it is being acted upon. The second is to do everything in our power in the physical plane to make sure it happens. And the third thing is to trust that however long it takes, the best and highest result will come.

Trust implies that you do not waver in your request. I often use the example of the soprano whose high "C" note can shatter a crystal goblet. The goblet does not shatter instantly, but it must be acted upon long enough by the vocal vibrations until the crystal changes form by shattering.

Faith is the understanding that we are not nouns, after all, but verbs . . . that the energy or life force in us, our soul, is always in motion, acting and being acted upon. When we die we will move into another level of being far beyond the limitations of our current physical form (1 CORINTHIANS 15:42–44).

Faith is always and ultimately about relationship. Having faith causes us to remember that we are not alone but are connected to God through birth, choice, and discipline.

Faith also causes us to remember that we have a say in how life goes—that life doesn't have to just happen to us, but that we have the power and responsibility to cause good things to become real, both in our lives and in those of others.

Faith is prayer. Faith is action. Faith is trust. Faith is the essence of all the things we've hoped for, the evidence of things not seen.

FAITH

Faith is always and ultimately about relationship.

FAITH IS PRAYER.

FAITH IS ACTION.

FAITH IS TRUST.

LEADERSHIP

LEADERSHIP IS THE ABILITY TO GET OTHERS TO TAKE ACTION. AUTHOR WARREN BENNIS ONCE OBSERVED THAT THE REAL GENIUS OF A LEADER LIES NOT IN PERSONAL ACHIEVEMENT, BUT IN UNLEASHING OTHER PEOPLE'S TALENT. JESUS HAS LONG BEEN MY PERSONAL ROLE MODEL FOR LEADERSHIP BECAUSE HE WAS ABLE TO MOBILIZE A DIVERSE, CONTENTIOUS, AND SOMETIMES COWARDLY GROUP INTO A TEAM THAT WAS SO POWERFUL IT CHANGED THE WORLD.

Leaders must have at least these three personal qualities.

They must have *self-discipline*. Having self–discipline means that they know their strengths as well as their weaknesses. They also must be clear about their highest gifts and have a sense of personal mission. All the great leaders in history had very clear goals that they wanted to accomplish, whether it was Moses leading the Israelites out of slavery; Martin Luther King, Jr., fighting for civil rights; Mother Teresa lending dignity to the dying; or Mahatma Gandhi reclaiming India from British colonialism. Each of these leaders was given a singular task to accomplish, and they disciplined all of their energies into making it happen.

Leaders must also have *action skills*. Leaders see themselves as "turnaround specialists." They believe that they either are or have the solutions to problems. They are willing to act alone, if necessary, to cause change to occur, and they're also strong enough to stand alone if others desert them when the task becomes too difficult

And leaders have *relationship skills*. Leaders are able to identify and ignite the highest dreams, aspirations, and actions in others. Moral leaders truly love the people they serve and see them not as means to an end, but as the very end themselves. Jesus spoke of his accomplishments on earth not as the miracles he performed but of the people he transformed. "My Father gave them to me," he said, "No one can snatch them from his hands" (JOHN 10:29 CEV). He also, amazingly enough, saw the people he served as his reward and asked that they go with him into paradise (JOHN 17:24). Not gold or silver, treasure or fame did he seek, but people—seeing them as divine gifts to him from God.

This is how leaders view people and how true leaders lead.

Leaders do four basic things with those they lead. First, they *excite* them about the big picture. Second, they *ground* them about the realities of what it will cost them to get there. Third, they *transform* them in such a way that the people are not the same—in capabilities, training, and courage—as they were when they encountered the leader. And fourth, leaders *release* people to do what they have been excited, grounded, and transformed to do. Very simple principles. Harness these understandings around leadership and you can accomplish anything.

LEADERSHIP IS THE ABILITY
to get others to take action.

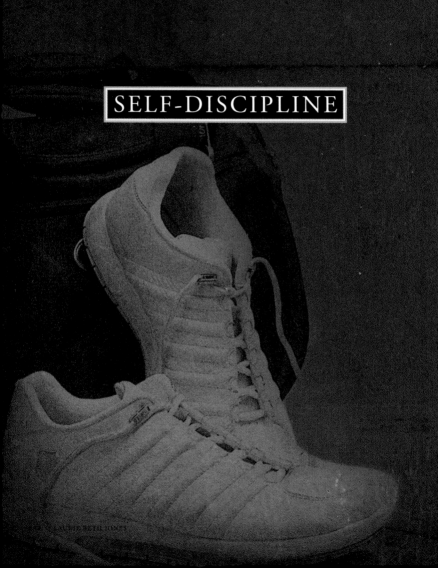

SELF-DISCIPLINE

One of my favorite proverbs reveals that "discipline has purple reins." Purple has long been used as a color to denote royalty, so the implication is that those who discipline themselves will become like royalty because of their self–restraint.

One of the leadership characteristics that Jesus demonstrated was his own self–discipline. Imagine . . . here was someone who had all the power in the universe to do whatever he wanted, and he very deliberately and carefully chose to do only what was his Father's will. He never acted out of self–interest, laziness, greed, or ambition. In the wilderness experience he got very clear about who he was and what he was called to do, and he did only that.

Today we are surrounded by hundreds of thousands of distractions, temptations, opportunities, and decisions about how and where we spend our time, our talents, and our energies. One of the top three characteristics most required for success is self–discipline. Leaders can have other characteristics or traits in abundance, yet still fail miserably and ultimately if they lack self–discipline.

Self–discipline means first of all that you harness your thoughts. Whatever you focus on, you will become. Letting your thoughts be filled with random, unfiltered messages leaves you open to others' programming, whether it be advertisers bombarding you with messages about their products or people whose agenda is to get you to do what is in their best interests, not necessarily your own. Consider your mind a precious kingdom or queendom and watch which thoughts you let in the gates, knowing that those thoughts will bring their friends and multiply.

The other form of self–discipline is physical. If we let our physical appetites rule us, we are no better than the animals. Indeed, animals in the wild often show more discipline than we do; for instance, very few will eat when they are not hungry. Listen to your body and be gentle with it, respecting it for the precious vessel that it is. Yet never let it rule you, or its appetites can squander and suffocate the treasures that are your mind and spirit.

Spirituality is not only a privilege, it is also a discipline. Jesus often went alone to pray—to reconnect with his divine source. Making time to be quiet and alone with God is something that does not just happen—it must be decided and acted upon. Discipline often means doing the same thing over and over again with the knowledge that eventually those little repeated actions will become habits that lead to the desired goal.

Another form of self–discipline is that of controlling your tongue and your temper. "Loose lips sink ships" was a saying during World War II that all military people and their families learned. It holds true today. Gossiping about others can gash holes in your own vessel. Letting loose a volley of angry words that can never be taken back has caused the end of many a career, marriage, and friendship. Your tongue is like a rudder on a ship. Be sure that wisdom is at the helm as you speak, and thus you will successfully sail toward your destination.

SELF-DISCIPLINE

Spirituality is not only a privilege, it is also a discipline.

SELF–DISCIPLINE MEANS

FIRST OF ALL THAT YOU HARNESS

YOUR THOUGHTS . . . THE OTHER FORM

OF SELF–DISCIPLINE IS PHYSICAL.

WISDOM

A certain passage about wisdom is so beautiful I have hand-written it on a note card and carried it with me for more than fifteen years. These excerpts that I meditate on are taken from chapter 7 of the Book of Wisdom, which scholars believe was written by King Solomon, as found in the New Jerusalem Bible. I consider the part of the passage that begins "for within her" the prettiest parade of words in the English language. Read them, and see if you agree.

"I prayed, and understanding was given me; I entreated, and the spirit of Wisdom came to me. I esteemed her more than scepters and thrones; compared with her, I held riches as nothing. I reckoned no precious stone to be her equal, for compared with her, all gold is a pinch of sand, and beside her, silver ranks as mud.

"I loved her more than health or beauty . . . In her company all good things came to me, and at her hands incalculable wealth. She is to human beings an inexhaustible treasure, and those who acquire this win God's friendship . . .

"For within her is a spirit intelligent, holy, unique, manifold, subtle, mobile, incisive, unsullied, lucid, invulnerable, benevolent, sharp, irresistible, beneficent, loving to all, steadfast, dependable, unperturbed, almighty, all–surveying, penetrating all intelligent, pure and most subtle spirits. For Wisdom is quicker to move than any motion; she is so pure, she pervades and permeates all things. She is a breath of the power of God, pure emanation of the glory of the Almighty; so nothing impure can find its way into her. She is a reflection of the eternal light, untarnished mirror of God's active power, and image of his goodness.

"Although she is alone, she can do everything. Herself unchanging, she renews the world . . . She indeed is more splendid than the sun, she outshines all the constellations; compared with light, she takes first place, for light must yield to night, but against Wisdom evil cannot prevail. Strong she reaches from one end of the world to the other, ordering all things for good."

I would challenge you to take each of the words mentioned here as descriptors of wisdom and make it your meditation word for an entire week. Imagine what the world would be like if everyone filled themselves with—and demonstrated— Wisdom such as this.

I hope to live those words in my life, and I would urge and challenge you to do the same.

'I PRAYED,

and understanding was given me;

I ENTREATED,

and the spirit of Wisdom came to me.'

CHARACTER

Many of us talk about character, but few of us seem to really know what this concept means. The word itself has Greek origins that mean "to engrave, as with a pointed stake." A character can be a distinctive mark, any letter of the alphabet, a mystic symbol or emblem, a code or cipher, or a distinctive trait. What we most consider it to be is "a pattern of behavior or personality found in an individual or group; moral constitution," as *Webster's New Collegiate Dictionary* describes it.

I often enjoy going to foreign films in the afternoon, especially during the hot Phoenix summers. Foreign films offer a perspective on the world that is not the usual American formula.

One movie that haunts me still is a Korean director's fable about a young man who rows out to a small floating temple to learn about life. The movie is short on dialogue and big on imagery, and the image that stays with me most is that of the Buddhist monk using a cat's tail, dipped in ink, to write a very long list of "characters" on the wooden floor that is their home. The monk's actions make no sense to the young man until he commits a crime. Upon his return the monk has the young, impatient man take the knife he used to commit the crime and slowly carve the characters that once were written only in paint. It takes the young man many days to carve out each character, and in so doing his soul is reshaped.

What struck me was that our lives are like that . . . perhaps we are playing with a kitten's tail, not taking our actions seriously. But what we draw even lightly with our deeds will one day become our destiny, carved out in the very foundation which once supported us.

I wrote a short poem once that read, "Sin begins a kitten, toying with the yarn of our lives, and grows into the tiger ripping out our heart and eyes."

Character is an engraving etched by our daily actions, as well as our patterns of repeated behavior. Little deeds become carved into habits that eventually everyone can see and trace with their fingers.

Character is what is acted out in the darkness. Character is who you are when everyone else around you is pulling you in another direction. Character is your soul revealed.

Golfer Bobby Jones astounded the world of golf when he called a penalty stroke on himself during a world championship match. As he had been preparing to hit the ball out of the woods he accidentally tapped it. The judges didn't see it, and no one else saw it either. "I saw it," he said, and with that admission and extra stroke, he lost the tournament he had been preparing for all year. When reporters questioned him later about why he did that, he said, "If I have a choice between winning a tournament or losing my honor, I'll choose to keep my honor every time." That is character.

Character was recently demonstrated by a poor woman in Pakistan. Lured into a field for what she thought was a traditional tribal ceremony, she was physically and sexually assaulted by the village men in retribution for an imagined slight her younger brother had committed. When a holy man reported this heinous act to the authorities, there was a world-wide uproar. The men who perpetrated the crime against her under the cloak of "tribal authority" were arrested, and she was awarded $6,500 to help her start a new life.

Rather than take what amounted to twenty years' worth of salary, she instead used her award to open a school in her village. She said, "The best way to fight violence and ignorance is education. I want every young girl in my village to be able to look any man in the eye and be proud." She is now raising funds to build a hospital for women.

When dark times come, character is revealed. This woman's character shines like a light in the darkness. Trouble didn't crush her—it merely revealed who she really was on the inside.

Character is the setting that allows your soul to shine.

'Sin begins a kitten, toying with the yarn of our lives, and grows into the tiger ripping out our heart and eyes.'

Character is your soul revealed.

INTEGRITY

When I ask adults to choose a core value that most represents who they are or want to become, many will choose the word "integrity." I often joke that they probably copied the word from their neighbors' notes because it is such a popular word. In one of my training seminars I asked the fourteen people who had chosen "integrity" as their core value to write their personal definitions of the concept. None of them could.

I believe it is wise for us to consider the root of the word "integrity," and what it means in a dictionary, as well as what it means in us.

Integrity is the quality or state of being complete, unbroken, whole, entire. The state or quality of being in perfect condition . . . of being of sound moral principle, upright, honest, and sincere. The root word is the Latin *integer*, which means "untouched, whole, entire."

Think for a moment about the word "unbroken."

How many unbroken people have you encountered in life? Perhaps like you, I have met people who had burdens to carry that would sink lesser souls, yet they moved through life gracefully and graciously. I also have encountered, as you have, people who seemed to have it all on the outside yet were broken on the inside.

What are the events and choices that break us? Do events and people break us, or do we break ourselves through how we choose to respond? In Mel Gibson's movie *The Passion of the Christ* we are shown that Christ was beaten and battered and physically broken. Yet through all that he maintained integrity—through all that he remained unbroken on the inside. This evening's paper showed a close-up of handcuffs on a famous CEO whose choices and actions caused thousands of people to lose both their jobs and their life savings. The CEO was wearing a thousand-dollar suit, driving a luxury car, living in one of many mansions that he and his wife owned around the world, and he seemed to have it all. His hair was combed. His face was clean. Yet he was all broken inside. He had no integrity.

Think about what it would look like for you to be unbroken, no matter what events may have taken place around you.

Integrity is the quality or state of being complete, unbroken.

Think about what it would look like for you to be unbroken, no matter what events may have taken place around you.

PRIORITIES

I remember the day that my mentor, Catherine Calhoun, sat down with me and showed me that life doesn't just happen, but that we can make choices and decide how it is to be lived. Even though I had been raised as a person of faith, I some-times confused "waiting on God" with just "waiting," period. In doing so I perhaps missed many opportunities presented to me.

In my book *Jesus, CEO* I recount a scene from the movie *Lawrence of Arabia*. A camel boy is discovered missing after a long journey. The group sadly decides, "It was written by Allah that the boy must die." Their belief causes them to shake their heads and go about their business. Lawrence, however, quickly remounts his camel and heads out into the searing heat. Three days later he returns with the nearly dead, but still alive, boy. As they both stumble toward the water, Lawrence tells the astonished crowd, "Nothing is written unless you and I write it."

The author Henry Miller wrote that for most of us, "Life is one long postponement." Too many of us wait to let others decide our fates. We let our priorities be about things that don't matter, and we let others decide the big questions for us. Napoleon Bonaparte said, "Nothing is more difficult, and thus more precious, than to be able to decide."

Freedom is not freedom *from* making decisions, but the freedom *for* making decisions. Jesus said, "By their fruits, ye shall know them" (MATTHEW 7:20 KJV). Whatever we think about, we bear on our branches. Whatever we put first in our lives, shows.

How we spend our money, how we spend our time, how we spend our talents . . . all are clear demonstrations about what we hold dear.

Set your mind on things above, not below. Seek first the kingdom of righteousness, and all else will be added to you. (MATTHEW 6:33).

Setting priorities: It's all about what goes at the top, and bottom, of your to–do lists.

PRIORITIES

LIFE DOESN'T JUST HAPPEN . . .

we can make choices and decide

how it is to be lived.

JUSTICE

A NUN IN NEW ORLEANS TOLD ME THAT
EVERY ONE OF US HAS BEEN GIVEN THE
SAME MISSION STATEMENT. SHE QUOTED
A FAVORITE VERSE OF MINE, MICAH 6:8,
WHICH READS, "WHAT DOES THE LORD
REQUIRE OF THEE, BUT TO DO JUSTLY,
AND TO LOVE MERCY, AND TO WALK
HUMBLY WITH THY GOD?"

This simple statement spoken by a prophet years ago highlights the Big Three in God's kingdom: justice, mercy, and humility.

One of our modern–day prophets, Martin Luther King, Jr., wrote these words from his Alabama jail cell in April of 1963: "Injustice anywhere is a threat to justice everywhere." So what exactly is justice?

A statue outside many of our courthouses shows a blindfolded woman with a scale in one hand and a sword in the other. According to the dictionary, justice is "sound reason, the quality of being right or correct, the use of authority and power to uphold what is right, just or lawful." The dictionary also defines justice as fairness, fair play, impartiality, uprightness, righteousness, virtue. Indeed, Cicero observed in 44 B.C. that "Justice is the crowning glory of the virtues."

Aristotle wrote, "All virtue is summed up in dealing justly," and Benjamin Disraeli declared, "Justice is truth in action."

To me, justice is a principle that demands everyone be treated fairly and equally. President Abraham Lincoln declared, "Those who would deny freedom to others deserve it not for themselves."

Laws are not always just. History has shown that at times many inhumane and unjust conditions were sanctioned by unjust laws written by people in power. Yet Jesus taught that there is a higher law of compassion, mercy, and the understanding that whatever one gives out, one will also reap.

Justice is the great leveler of power. By enforcing the truth that all people are equal, justice gives rise to the brightness within us and also protects us from our shadowed selves.

JUSTICE GIVES RISE TO THE BRIGHTNESS WITHIN US AND ALSO PROTECTS US FROM OUR SHADOWED SELVES.

JUSTICE

'Injustice anywhere is a threat to justice everywhere.'

MARTIN LUTHER KING, JR.

DIGNITY

It has been said that dignity is a possession that only you can throw away. Jesus lamented that we seem to not understand our high birth and calling, saying, "In your Scriptures doesn't God say, 'You are gods'?" (JOHN 10:34 CEV). We are among the highest of God's creations. We like to think that we are God's crowning achievement, and many times we are. How we perceive ourselves, and our place in heaven, often determines how others view us.

Perhaps you have noticed a person who carries himself or herself with a sense of royalty and honor.

Yet every day we are exposed to people who have forgotten their dignity or traded it in for whatever form of attention a camera or a crowd can render.

I often think that if someone were to challenge me to identify Jesus' core values, treating others with dignity and respect would have to be among them. He looked at people and saw the potential greatness in them. To those who were humble, he offered a lift up. To those who thought themselves to be superior, he used strong words and actions to overcome their presuppositions.

Through his actions Jesus taught that arrogance is not dignity.

Dignity is humility cloaked in love. It is the divine remembrance. It is the waking acknowledgement of the invitation we have all received—to walk and sit with God.

Dignity is one gift we are all equally given, and it is one gift that only we ourselves can throw away. If you guard your dignity, and that of others, you will be doing the work of God.

Dignity is humility cloaked in love . . . If you guard your dignity, and that of others, you will be doing the work of God.

KINDNESS

Kindness is one of my favorite words because it is my sister Kathy's core value. Her mission statement reads that she wants to "ascend to Christ through acts of beauty and kindness." I am pleased to say that this is indeed how she lives and who she is. She is the first one to consider the feelings of others, no matter how insignificant they seem.

She uses her considerable artistic talents to write handmade sympathy cards to neighbors who have lost loved ones or to highlight beautiful memories through paintings. Perhaps she learned this quality through our mother, who once turned her grief for a neighbor's lost son into a painting of him, which she gave to the grieving parents. My mother would also sit and sing lullabies to a young man abandoned by his family as he died of AIDS.

Kindness is the quality of using your time, energy, and talents to make life better for someone else, if only for a moment. Jesus said that even if you simply bring a cup of water to someone in his name, your act of kindness will be remembered and recorded through all eternity (MARK 9:41).

Kindness is a quiet virtue. It is not usually heralded in our society, which worships fame and beauty, success and material wealth, power and good fortune. Kindness gives when others grasp. Kindness listens when others shout.

Kindness bows its head in prayer when others are raising their fists. Kindness takes the low road, sometimes, and is willing to walk through the valley of the shadow of death if it means someone else won't have to walk it alone.

Kindness is a suspension of self–care, self–thought, self anything. Kindness sees only the need of the other, and in so doing, has the eyes of God.

Kindness

KINDNESS IS THE QUALITY OF

USING YOUR TIME, ENERGY, AND

TALENTS TO MAKE LIFE BETTER

FOR SOMEONE ELSE.

COMMUNITY

Community means "all of the people living in a particular district, city, or other defined area; or the district, city, or other defined area where they live." It also means "a group of people forming a smaller social unity with a larger one, and sharing common interest, work, identity, and location." Its root word also signifies fellowship.

There is something in us that causes us to cluster; it is not in the nature of humanity to want to be alone. In America we prize our individual liberty so much that I often wonder if we have lost the art and grounding of community. I am often tickled when I see people sitting alone at lunch while talking on their cell phones to others. It seems no matter where we are, something in us wants to reach out and touch somebody—to connect.

We've all heard the saying, "It takes a village to raise a child." But who and where is that village now?

As we live in suburbs where garage doors open up and swallow the people into their isolated confines, how do we get to know our neighbors? When Jesus said, "Love your neighbor as yourself" (MATTHEW 22:39), he was implying that you need to take time to get to know your neighbors.

I regret that we have lost front porches, village squares, and town meetings. Much humanity has been lost because of our automatic garage doors. Yet the internet is providing us with ways to engage in new communities through technology—where instantly we can connect with others of like mind and similar interests and concerns.

I say all this because no one can thrive outside of some kind of caring network of others. It is said that if we died tomorrow most of us would have about two hundred fifty people attend our funeral. These people were somehow part of our web of interactions, and somehow, for better or worse, we touched their lives.

How beautiful it is for people to dwell together in harmony (PSALM 133:1).

Ah, the vision of the ancients. It is one that we can create here and now, as well.

It is wise to build a community that will support you when you are sick and to which you can contribute when you are well. We each have the breath of the other in us. Recognize that, and sing together, and Jesus himself will come dwell with you.

No one can thrive outside
of some kind of caring
network of others.

We each have the breath of the other in us.

EXCELLENCE

TO EXCEL MEANS TO STAND

APART, TO BE ABOVE THE NORM,

TO EXCEED EXPECTATIONS.

We live in a world and a culture where it seems we are expected to be excellent in all things. We must be physically fit, morally tempered, financially sound, good to our neighbors, patriotic, spiritually enlightened, and highly fashionable, to boot. Some among us become overachievers, aiming for perfection in every area. Some of us, overwhelmed and discouraged by the demands, opt out altogether and choose to spend our lives blaming others for our mediocrity. Yet life is really a series of decisions about where we choose to excel.

I read a quote once that observed, "There is no such thing as real failure, because even failure serves as a great example of what not to do."

I believe we must choose the spheres where we are to be excellent based on our mission and our values. Jesus challenged us to excel in the things of heaven and leave the lesser things behind. Every strength has a corresponding weakness, so it is wise to understand that when we choose to excel in some things, we will not do as well in others.

People who are often held up as examples of "success" may be total failures in matters of relationship or self–discipline. Jesus challenged people to consider how much it really matters if someone gains the whole world—achieves success —yet loses his or her own soul (MATTHEW 16:26).

Do not confuse success with excellence. Do not confuse fame or wealth with excellence, either. Nor should you believe that you cannot have all of the above due to your excellent pursuit of heavenly matters.

Joseph of the Old Testament excelled in administration (GENESIS 39–41). He practiced excellence whether he was in a prison or a palace. It was his guiding principle, and it brought him to a position of immense power in the land.

There is a proverb that reads, "Your gift will bring you before kings."

Identify your personal areas of excellence. Ask your friends and family members what you are really good at, and then get better at those things. Craftsmanship is determined by the fine attention to detail, such as the many extra coats of varnish or polish that take a product to an extraordinary level of shine.

Excellence comes from extra effort. There is neither an easy way nor shortcut there. The hours spent alone, honing one's craft, make the difference between a seat before kings or a barstool among beggars.

One of my friend's favorite movie lines is from a Marlon Brando film called *On the Waterfront*. Brando's character laments in the final scene, "I could'a been a contender." The tale ends with the viewer pondering the roads not taken, the gifts not identified or developed or polished.

Regret and excellence walk two different paths, and excellence always chooses the one that goes uphill.

EXCELLENCE

Life is a series of decisions about where we choose to excel.

LOYALTY

One of my neighbors had a darling little girl who seemed ahead of her years. She was blessed to be born to parents who had her late in life and thus saw her as the gift that she was. One day my neighbors got an invitation to "Amanda's Wedding." Thinking that a wedding for a six–year–old girl was bound to be an interesting affair, they decided they couldn't miss it.

Showing up at the proper time, they were delighted to see a gathering of the adults and children in the neighborhood, all properly dressed for the occasion. Amanda's father had built her an arbor of roses and was dressed in a tuxedo as he solemnly walked her down the lane in the beautiful backyard.

Eager to know who the groom was, the guests craned their necks to see who was waiting for her. Not seeing anyone, they decided there might be a surprise in store. They were correct. When her father had walked her down the aisle, he turned with her to face the crowd and said, "Amanda asked for a wedding today, and this is what she wants to say."

Amanda got out a piece of paper, unfolded it, and began to read:

"Today, I, Amanda Jenkins, do solemnly pledge to be true to myself. I promise to always remember the dreams I am having right now in my childhood and to never let anyone or anything take them away. I promise to take care of myself and to love others, but to always remember that nobody can give me something that I cannot give myself."

With that, she beamed, tossed her bouquet into the audience, and ran laughing down the aisle as everyone threw birdseed from the packets that had been prepared.

I think about the wisdom of parents who saw the longing of a child's heart for a meaningful ceremony and had her wed her own dreams. They were teaching her a loyalty to principles, to dreams, to innocence, to responsibility—the kind of loyalty that can never be betrayed by others but only forsaken by oneself.

Perhaps you, like I, have seen loyalty abused. Battered wives who refuse to leave their husbands, Nazi soldiers, and terrorists all have a misplaced loyalty that can be ignorant, maiming, and blind. It has struck me sadly that "loyalty" is one of the core values expressed among the gang members with whom we work in our Path4Teens programs. I remember asking a young girl who was incarcerated who she was loyal to, and she said, "My 'hood." I asked her what gifts that loyalty had brought her, and she put her head down and looked away.

Jesus loved all, yet pledged his loyalty to only God. He cared for others but was able to discern when those he loved urged him to take an easier path—away from his calling. Jesus quickly dismissed even his friend Peter when he urged him to be loyal to anything but doing God's will.

When your loyalty is called into question, discern who and what are really challenging you. If the action being required of you is not of the highest order, then you are not being challenged by loyalty but by peer pressure or fear.

Loyalty is love with a price. And the price of that love is discernment.

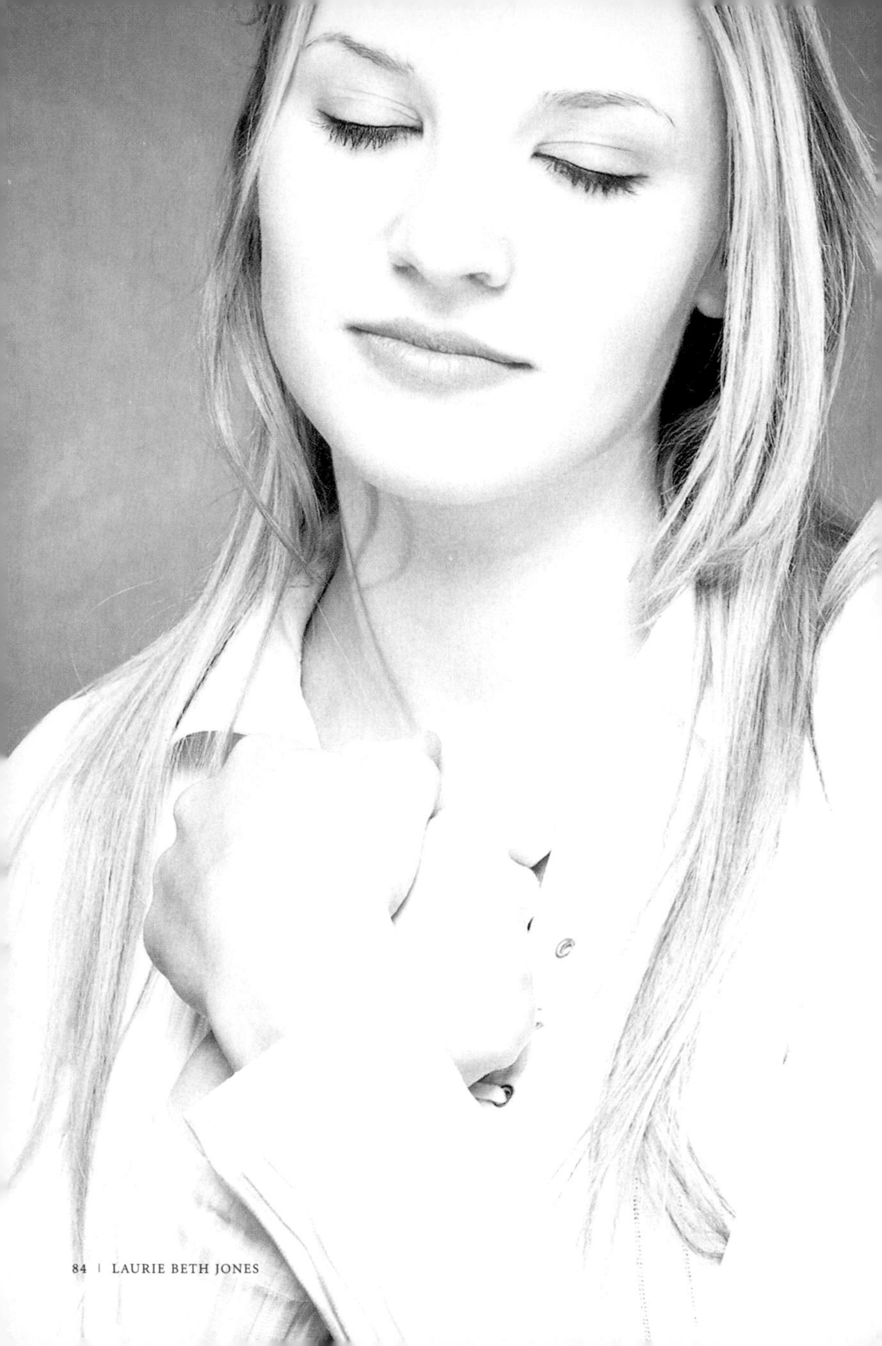

Loyalty

LOYALTY IS LOVE WITH A PRICE.

AND THE PRICE OF THAT LOVE

IS DISCERNMENT.

'I pledge to be true to myself. I promise
to always remember the dreams I am having
right now in my childhood and to never let
anyone or anything take them away.'

MORALITY

John Milton wrote, "License they mean when they cry liberty."

"Morality" is often a word we use when someone else's actions have offended us, yet we seldom apply this word equally to ourselves.

When Jesus said, "If any of you have never sinned, then go ahead and throw the first stone at her!" (JOHN 8:7 CEV), he was not condoning the improper actions of the woman before him. He was establishing a foundation of compassion and repentance for all social judgments.

I was tickled to overhear someone at a party say, "The more he talked of morality, the more we clung to our daughters."

More than one event has shown that all too often those who speak the loudest about morality are those with hidden issues around it.

True morality wears plain clothes and needs no spokesperson, introduction, or defense. It is the best of the Golden Rule: "Do unto others as you would have them do unto you." It is considering the consequences to others of one's individual actions, and it is the willingness to bear the consequences of those deeds.

It is bearing respect for one's own body, as well as those of others. True morality does no harm.

Psychologist Erich Fromm wrote, "The basic condition for morality is the ability to preserve one's integrity against power."

Morality means answering to the higher, hidden laws of God. People who owned slaves, for example, were not breaking any human law at the time, but most surely were immoral in God's eyes. The woman caught in adultery was (for)given a clean slate upon her repentance (JOHN 8:1–11), while Jesus called the outwardly perfect Pharisees "tombs of decay" (MATTHEW 23:27).

I once toured an incredible exhibit about ancient Egypt in the New York Museum of Natural History. While there I learned the Egyptians believed that upon your death, your heart would be weighed on a scale, and depending on its purity you would either receive or be denied passage into the next life. Morality is a weighing of the heart that has nothing to do with written laws. It is only the scales, God, and you.

No laws can shield you or excuses blind you.

Morality is the weighing of your heart upon the heavenly scale.

MORALITY

. . . IS BEARING RESPECT

FOR ONE'S OWN BODY, AS WELL

AS THOSE OF OTHERS.

TRUE MORALITY DOES NO HARM.

HONESTY

THE FIRST U.S. PRESIDENT, GEORGE
WASHINGTON, ONCE SAID, "HONESTY IS
THE BEST POLICY, BOTH IN GOVERN-
MENT, AND IN ONE'S PRIVATE DEALINGS."
HONESTY, TRUTH, AND INTEGRITY ARE
VALUES THAT ARE INTERTWINED.

Sir Walter Scott wrote, "Oh what a tangled web we weave, when first we practice to deceive."

Jesus said, "The truth shall make you free" (JOHN 8:32 NKJV). I have long pondered that six–word promise. What did he mean by that? Something in us knows we harm ourselves and others by not telling the truth, and yet we do it anyway. Sometimes lying seems easier, and besides, everyone else is doing it, one might say. But what is the cost?

So much heartache in this world is caused by people not being honest with themselves or with others. The hardest person to be honest with is yourself. So often we surround ourselves with people who say what we want to hear but who have only their own good in mind. A person who will tell you the truth, without regard for the consequences, is really the one who helps you the most, even if there is a little sting attached.

Perhaps you grew up hearing the story of "The Emperor's New Clothes." A vain emperor held a procession to show off his beautiful new suit supposedly made from cloth that couldn't be seen by fools. Of course, the emperor had been swindled—his clothes did not, in fact, exist—but neither he nor anyone else had the courage to be honest and say, "I can't see the clothes," because no one wanted to be thought a fool. Instead, they all pretended that the emperor was wearing a wonderful outfit and would openly praise him for his wardrobe. One day a child in the crowd called out the obvious, saying, "Mommy, that man is naked!" There was a hush over the crowd as the emperor was forced to face the fact that indeed he had no clothes. It took the innocence and fearlessness of a child to tell him the truth.

Adrienne Rich wrote, "When a woman tells the truth she is creating the possibility of more truth around her." People with substance addictions are often forced to face the truth about themselves the hard way. They call it "hitting bottom." Healing sometimes only begins when people admit their problem honestly and begin to ask for help.

Jesus openly confronted people and encouraged them to be honest about their situations. He did this not to make them feel bad, but to let them realize the gap between where they were and where they wanted to be.

It takes courage to be honest. Sometimes the truth hurts.

But lies enter like a worm and spread throughout an oak tree, ultimately bringing about the downfall of even the largest enterprises.

Alexander Pope said, "An honest human being is the noblest work of God." I believe God must give you the courage to be honest, but only you can stay that way.

Truth and freedom go hand in hand, and it is a bond that cannot be broken.

Honesty

*So much heartache in this world
is caused by people not being honest
with themselves or with others.*

TRUTH AND FREEDOM GO HAND IN HAND,
and it is a bond that cannot be broken.

SELF-WORTH

The ancient Basques in Spain had a ritual they did with their youth. Before they would allow their young people to face the world as adults, they would take them into a cave and shout at them from the corners. "Who are you? What are you worth?" The young people in the cave then would have to boldly proclaim their gifts and their worth. If anyone could not state their own strengths, they were assigned to spend another year with the elders and learn more about themselves.

It is said that 85 percent of all our self–talk is negative. I continue to be amazed by people who are successful in every area of life but who still berate themselves for not being good enough. In my Path training seminars I often challenge people, "I will pay anyone in this room one thousand dollars if they can find a scripture where Jesus ever said one negative thing about himself." Nobody has ever been able to take me up on it. You might say, "Sure, but he was the Son of God. Of course he wouldn't say anything negative about himself." But he also told us to do as he did, right?

If you ever listen to champions being interviewed after a loss, you will notice that usually they still praise themselves.

Their coaches know that putting yourself down doesn't get you anywhere but down.

Knowing that you are loved and cherished and treasured and valued is a gift that each of us deserve. Yet if self–worth wasn't instilled in you from birth, you can still achieve it simply by virtue of the fact that you exist. You are a triumph of genealogy, science, spirit, and history. You are the shining star on the family tree. Being alive is an accomplishment in itself, as is staying alive. The fact that you have been given this book, probably because you have graduated recently, means that you have the ability to set goals and follow through on them, which makes you a winner.

If you think your self–worth is attached to anything you own, or do, or accomplish, or achieve, you will always be looking over your shoulder—afraid to lose, afraid to fail, afraid to be stolen from.

Your worth is established at birth. Love yourself for being alive. Love yourself for being unique. Love yourself for having dreams. And love yourself for loving others.

If someone is shouting at you from the darkness of a cave—saying, "Who are you? What are you worth?"—be able to answer them proudly and walk into the sunshine.

PUTTING YOURSELF DOWN
DOESN'T GET YOU ANYWHERE
BUT DOWN.

PERSEVERANCE

IT HAS BEEN SAID, "THE MOST
VALUABLE THING IN THE WORLD
ISN'T TALENT OR WEALTH, BEAUTY
OR INTELLIGENCE. IT IS THE ABILITY
TO PERSEVERE."

Being able to stick to a task and finish it will lead to success in almost any endeavor. Jesus said that whoever puts their hand to the plow, and then hesitates, is not fit for the kingdom of heaven (LUKE 9:62). He was saying that only those who are willing to go the distance are worthy of a place in paradise.

It is a lot easier to begin something than to finish it.

The story is told of a snail that very slowly crawls up the steps to a front porch. A little boy, with nothing better to do, picks up the snail and hurls it out into the meadow. Three years later the snail returns. The boy, not so little anymore, picks up the snail in astonishment. The snail raises itself up, looks at the boy, and asks, "What was that about?"

Once you are convinced of the rightness of your task, never give up. It may be that you are only seconds away from victory when you feel the most discouraged and tired.

A friend of mine named Ed has gained a reputation as an avid cyclist. Even though he is in his sixties, he still often wins forty–mile races against much younger men. When I asked him one day how he did it, he said, "I figure that the person ahead of me is hurting just as much as I am, so if I give it one more ounce I just might take him." And he usually does.

It is the last drop of a thousand that causes the cup to overflow. Which drop is more valuable than the other?

It is the accumulated efforts and patience that create masterpieces. So even if life picks you up and hurls you into a meadow, persevere until it picks you up again.

This time, you'll be the one smiling.

Being able to stick to a task and finish it will lead to success in almost any endeavor.

ONCE YOU ARE

CONVINCED OF THE

RIGHTNESS OF YOUR

TASK, NEVER GIVE UP.

SERVICE

The great humanitarian Albert Schweitzer said, "You will only have happiness when you have sought, and found, how to serve."

Schweitzer came from a family of great wealth. As such he was able to study music in Germany. He became a world-famous pianist, as well as a medical doctor. Yet something in his heart told him there was more to life. One day he went to help with the lepers in Africa, where he saw a need so great that he dedicated his life to helping people there. In the process, he built a renowned health clinic and earned a Nobel Peace Prize.

He could have chosen wealth, fame, and a life of leisure.

But Schweitzer said he was blessed because he found how and where to serve.

Serving others out of choice, rather than compunction, is a very freeing feeling. When you are living your gifts at your highest level, then you will be serving others. When you lose yourself in the task at hand, and are willing to sacrifice comfort in order to fulfill your purpose, you are in bliss.

Finding and living your mission is, indeed, the only path to joy. To fulfill your purpose on this earth is the greatest gift you could give anyone, especially yourself.

Learn this formula well:

Multiply joy by subtracting sorrow.

Divide burdens by adding support.

This math will make you wiser than any algebra you know.

Jesus said he came not to be served, but to serve (MATTHEW 20:28).

The path of life awaits you. You have been trained, gifted, blessed, and encouraged. Now go out and make a difference . . . as only you can.

Blessings to you,

Laurie Beth Jones

Go out and make a difference . . .

as only you can.

PERSONAL NOTES

to the Graduate From God

(Scriptures taken from the New Century Version)

FREEDOM

So I will live in freedom, because I want to follow your orders.

PSALM 119:45

So Jesus said to the Jews who believed in him, "If you continue to obey my teaching, you are truly my followers. Then you will know the truth, and the truth will make you free . . . . So if the Son makes you free, you will be truly free."

JOHN 8:31-32, 36

In the past you were slaves to sin— sin controlled you. But thank God, you fully obeyed the things that you were taught. You were made free from sin, and now you are slaves to goodness.

ROMANS 6:17, 18

"I am allowed to do all things," but all things are not good for me to do. "I am allowed to do all things," but I will not let anything make me its slave . . . "We are allowed to do all things," but all things are not good for us to do. "We are allowed to do all things," but not all things help others grow stronger. Do not look out only for yourselves. Look out for the good of others also.

1 CORINTHIANS 6:12; 10:23, 24

We have freedom now, because Christ made us free. So stand strong . . . My brothers and sisters, God called you to be free, but do not use your freedom as an excuse to do what pleases your sinful self. Serve each other with love.

GALATIANS 5:1, 13

RESPECT

Peter began to speak: "I really understand now that to God every person is the same. In every country God accepts anyone who worships him and does what is right."

ACTS 10:34, 35

Live as free people, but do not use your freedom as an excuse to do evil. Live as servants of God. Show respect for all people: Love the brothers and sisters of God's family, respect God, honor the king.

1 PETER 2:16, 17

Love each other like brothers and sisters. Give each other more honor than you want for yourselves.

ROMANS 12:10

I am the LORD your God. Keep yourselves holy for me because I am holy.

LEVITICUS 11:44

LORD, who may enter your Holy Tent?
Who may live on your holy mountain?
Only those who are innocent
and who do what is right.
Such people speak the truth from their hearts and do not tell lies about others.
They do no wrong to their neighbors and do not gossip.
They do not respect hateful people but honor those who honor the LORD.
They keep their promises to their neighbors,
even when it hurts.
They do not charge interest on money they lend
and do not take money to hurt innocent people.
Whoever does all these things will never be destroyed.

PSALM 15:1-5

"The LORD himself will go before you. He will be with you;
he will not leave you or forget you.
Don't be afraid and don't worry."

DEUTERONOMY 31:8

"I will be with you. I will not leave you or forget you . . . . be strong and brave! You must lead these people . . . Be strong and brave . . . . Always remember what is written in the Book of the Teachings. Study it day and night to be sure to obey everything that is written there. If you do this, you will be wise and successful in everything. Remember that I commanded you to be strong and brave. Don't be afraid, because the LORD your God will be with you everywhere you go."

JOSHUA 1:5-9

Evil people run even though no one is chasing them, but good people are as brave as a lion.

PROVERBS 28:1

God did not give us a spirit that makes us afraid but a spirit of power and love and self-control.

2 TIMOTHY 1:7

FRIENDSHIP

Whoever forgives someone's sin
makes a friend,
but gossiping about the sin
breaks up friendships.

PROVERBS 17:9

Some friends may ruin you,
but a real friend will be more
loyal than a brother.

PROVERBS 18:24

Don't forget your friend or your
parent's friend.
Don't always go to your family
for help when trouble comes.
A neighbor close by is better
than a family far away.

PROVERBS 27:10

Spend time with the wise
and you will become wise,
but the friends of fools
will suffer.

PROVERBS 13:20

Two people are better than one,
because they get more done by
working together.
If one falls down,
the other can help him up.
But it is bad for the person who
is alone and falls,
because no one is there to help.
If two lie down together, they
will be warm,
but a person alone will not be
warm.
An enemy might defeat one
person,
but two people together can
defend themselves;
a rope that is woven of three
strings is hard to break.

ECCLESIASTES 4:9-12

HUMILITY

Though the LORD is supreme,
he takes care of those who are
humble, but he stays away from
the proud.

PSALM 138:6

Pride leads only to shame;
it is wise to be humble.

PROVERBS 11:2

Fools think they are doing right,
but the wise listen to advice.

PROVERBS 12:15

Respect for the LORD will teach
you wisdom.
If you want to be honored,
you must be humble.

PROVERBS 15:33

And this is the reason: God lives
forever and is holy.
He is high and lifted up.
He says, "I live in a high and
holy place,
but I also live with people who
are sad and humble.
I give new life to those who are
humble
and to those whose hearts are
broken."

ISAIAH 57:15

"Accept my teachings and learn
from me, because I am gentle
and humble in spirit, and you
will find rest for your lives."

MATTHEW 11:29

"Whoever wants to become the
first among you must serve all
of you like a slave. In the same
way, the Son of Man did not
come to be served. He came to
serve others and to give his life
as a ransom for many people."

MARK 10:44, 45

Trust the LORD with all your heart, and don't depend on your own understanding. Remember the LORD in all you do, and he will give you success.

PROVERBS 3:5, 6

Guard what God has trusted to you. Stay away from foolish, useless talk and from the arguments of what is falsely called "knowledge." By saying they have that "knowledge," some have missed the true faith. Grace be with you.

1 TIMOTHY 6:20, 21

"I tell you the truth, you can say to this mountain, 'Go, fall into the sea.' And if you have no doubts in your mind and believe that what you say will happen, God will do it for you. So I tell you to believe that you have received the things you ask for in prayer, and God will give them to you."

MARK 11:23, 24

Since we have been made right with God by our faith, we have peace with God. This happened through our Lord Jesus Christ.

ROMANS 5:1

Faith means being sure of the things we hope for and knowing that something is real even if we do not see it . . . Without faith no one can please God. Anyone who comes to God must believe that he is real and that he rewards those who truly want to find him.

HEBREWS 11:1, 6

My brothers and sisters, if people say they have faith, but do nothing, their faith is worth nothing. Can faith like that save them? . . . Faith that is alone—that does nothing—is dead. Someone might say, "You have faith, but I have deeds." Show me your faith without doing anything, and I will show you my faith by what I do . . . Just as a person's body that does not have a spirit is dead, so faith that does nothing is dead!

JAMES 2:14, 17, 18, 26

LEADERSHIP

"I cannot take care of your problems, your troubles, and your arguments by myself. So choose some men from each tribe—wise men who have understanding and experience—and I will make them leaders over you."

DEUTERONOMY 1:12, 13

"I ask that you give me an obedient heart so I can rule the people in the right way and will know the difference between right and wrong. Otherwise, it is impossible to rule this great people of yours."

1 KINGS 3:9

Without leadership a nation falls, but lots of good advice will save it.

PROVERBS 11:14

Hard workers will become leaders, but those who are lazy will be slaves.

PROVERBS 12:24

For the Lord's sake, yield to the people who have authority in this world: the king, who is the highest authority, and the leaders who are sent by him to punish those who do wrong and to praise those who do right.

1 PETER 2:13, 14

A king will rule in a way that
brings justice,
and leaders will make fair
decisions.
Then each ruler will be like a
shelter from the wind,
like a safe place in a storm,
like streams of water in a dry land,
like a cool shadow from a large
rock in a hot land.
People will look to the king for
help,
and they will truly listen to what
he says.
People who are now worried will
be able to understand.
Those who cannot speak clearly
now will then be able to speak
clearly and quickly . . .
A good leader plans to do good,
and those good things make him a
good leader.

ISAIAH 32:1-4, 8

SELF-DISCIPLINE

A lazy person will end up poor,
but a hard worker will become rich.
Those who gather crops on time
are wise, but those who sleep
through the harvest are a disgrace.

PROVERBS 10:4-5

Lazy people sleep a lot,
and idle people will go hungry.

PROVERBS 19:15

Those who drink and eat too much
become poor.
They sleep too much and end up
wearing rags . . .
Learn the truth and never reject it.
Get wisdom, self-control, and
understanding.

PROVERBS 23:19, 23

Be careful what you think, because
your thoughts run your life.
Don't use your mouth to tell lies;
don't ever say things that are not
true.
Keep your eyes focused on what is
right, and look straight ahead to
what is good.
Be careful what you do, and always
do what is right.

PROVERBS 4:23-26

Someone with a quick temper does
foolish things, but someone with
understanding remains calm.
Those who work hard make a profit, but those who only talk will be
poor.

PROVERBS 14:17, 23

WISDOM

The wise do what they are told,
but a talkative fool will be
ruined . . .
The wise don't tell everything they
know, but the foolish talk too
much and are ruined . . .
A foolish person enjoys doing
wrong, but a person with understanding enjoys doing what is wise.

PROVERBS 10:8, 14, 23

Good sense will protect you;
understanding will guard you.

PROVERBS 2:11

"Listen, I am sending you out like
sheep among wolves.
So be as smart as snakes and as
innocent as doves."

MATTHEW 10:16

CHARACTER

God has chosen you and made you his holy people. He loves you. So always do these things: Show mercy to others, be kind, humble, gentle, and patient. Get along with each other, and forgive each other. If someone does wrong to you, forgive that person because the Lord forgave you. Do all these things; but most important, love each other. Love is what holds you all together in perfect unity. Let the peace that Christ gives control your thinking, because you were all called together in one body to have peace. Always be thankful. Let the teaching of Christ live in you richly. Use all wisdom to teach and instruct each other by singing psalms, hymns, and spiritual songs with thankfulness in your hearts to God. Everything you do or say should be done to obey Jesus your Lord. And in all you do, give thanks to God the Father through Jesus.

COLOSSIANS 3:12-17

Being respected is more important than having great riches.
To be well thought of is better than silver or gold.
Respecting the LORD and not being proud
will bring you wealth, honor, and life.
Evil people's lives are like paths covered with thorns and traps.
People who guard themselves don't have such problems.
Train children how to live right, and when they are old, they will not change.
The rich rule over the poor, and borrowers are servants to lenders.
Those who plan evil will receive trouble.
Their cruel anger will come to an end.
Generous people will be blessed, because they share their food with the poor.
Get rid of the one who makes fun of wisdom.
Then fighting, quarrels, and insults will stop.
Whoever loves pure thoughts and kind words
will have even the king as a friend.

PROVERBS 22:1-11

INTEGRITY

Good people who live honest lives will be a blessing to their children.

PROVERBS 20:7

"I, the LORD, look into a person's heart and test the mind.
So I can decide what each one deserves; I can give each one the right payment for what he does."

JEREMIAH 17:10

We show we are servants of God by our pure lives, our understanding, patience, and kindness, by the Holy Spirit, by true love, by speaking the truth, and by God's power. We use our right living to defend ourselves against everything.

2 CORINTHIANS 6:6, 7

"Do to others what you would want them to do to you."

LUKE 6:31

"Whoever can be trusted with a little can also be trusted with a lot, and whoever is dishonest with a little is dishonest with a lot."

LUKE 16:10

Always be humble, gentle, and patient, accepting each other in love.

EPHESIANS 4:2

PERSONAL NOTES

PRIORITIES

Jesus answered, "'Love the Lord your God with all your heart, all your soul, and all your mind.' This is the first and most important command. And the second command is like the first: 'Love your neighbor as you love yourself.'"

MATTHEW 22:37-39

Jesus sat down and called the twelve apostles to him. He said, "Whoever wants to be the most important must be last of all and servant of all."

MARK 9:35

But the Lord answered her, "Martha, Martha, you are worried and upset about many things. Only one thing is important. Mary has chosen the better thing, and it will never be taken away from her."

LUKE 10:41, 42

I passed on to you what I received, of which this was most important: that Christ died for our sins, as the Scriptures say; that he was buried and was raised to life on the third day as the Scriptures say; and that he was seen by Peter and then by the twelve apostles.

1 CORINTHIANS 15:3-5

Most importantly, love each other deeply, because love will cause many sins to be forgiven.

1 PETER 4:8

In the kingdom of God, eating and drinking are not important. The important things are living right with God, peace, and joy in the Holy Spirit.

ROMANS 14:17

Wisdom is the most important thing; so get wisdom.
If it costs everything you have, get understanding.
Treasure wisdom, and it will make you great;
hold on to it, and it will bring you honor.

PROVERBS 4:7, 8

JUSTICE

"Be fair in your judging. You must not show special favor to poor people or great people, but be fair when you judge your neighbor."

LEVITICUS 19:15

He says, "How long will you defend evil people?
How long will you show greater kindness to the wicked?
Defend the weak and the orphans;
defend the rights of the poor and suffering.
Save the weak and helpless;
free them from the power of the wicked."

PSALM 82:2-4

The LORD hates both of these things: freeing the guilty and punishing the innocent.

PROVERBS 17:15

The person who tells one side of a story seems right,
until someone else comes and asks questions.

PROVERBS 18:17

"Stop judging by the way things look, but judge by what is really right."

JOHN 7:24

A person might have to suffer even when it is unfair, but if he thinks of God and stands the pain, God is pleased . . . If you suffer for doing good, and you are patient, then God is pleased.

1 PETER 2:19, 20

DIGNITY

Proud people will be ruined,
but the humble will be honored.
Anyone who answers without
listening
is foolish and confused.

PROVERBS 18:12, 13

Don't brag to the king
and act as if you are great.
It is better for him to give you a
higher position
than to bring you down in front
of the prince.

PROVERBS 25:6, 7

Don't praise yourself. Let
someone else do it.
Let the praise come from a
stranger and not from your own
mouth.

PROVERBS 27:2

Do not speak angrily to an older
man, but plead with him as if he
were your father. Treat younger
men like brothers, older women
like mothers, and younger
women like sisters. Always treat
them in a pure way.

1 TIMOTHY 5:1, 2

"Whoever makes himself great
will be made humble. Whoever
makes himself humble will be
made great."

MATTHEW 23:12

"The person who trusts in the
LORD will be blessed.
The LORD will show him that he
can be trusted.
He will be strong, like a tree
planted near water
that sends its roots by a stream.
It is not afraid when the days are
hot; its leaves are always green.
It does not worry in a year when
no rain comes;
it always produces fruit."

JEREMIAH 17:7, 8

Let everyone see that you are
gentle and kind. The Lord is
coming soon. Do not worry
about anything, but pray and
ask God for everything you
need, always giving thanks. And
God's peace, which is so great
we cannot understand it, will
keep your hearts and minds in
Christ Jesus.

PHILIPPIANS 4:5-7

Don't ever forget kindness and truth.
Wear them like a necklace.
Write them on your heart as if on a tablet.
Then you will be respected and will please both God and people.

PROVERBS 3:3, 4

It is a sin to hate your neighbor, but being kind to the needy brings happiness.
Those who make evil plans will be ruined,
but those who plan to do good will be loved and trusted.

PROVERBS 14:21, 22

"This is what the LORD All-Powerful says: 'Do what is right and true. Be kind and merciful to each other. Don't hurt widows and orphans, foreigners or the poor; don't even think of doing evil to somebody else.'"

ZECHARIAH 7:9, 10

"If you are nice only to your friends, you are no better than other people. Even those who don't know God are nice to their friends."

MATTHEW 5:47

By helping each other with your troubles, you truly obey the law of Christ.

GALATIANS 6:2

Do not be bitter or angry or mad. Never shout angrily or say things to hurt others. Never do anything evil. Be kind and loving to each other, and forgive each other just as God forgave you in Christ.

EPHESIANS 4:31, 32

When you talk, you should always be kind and pleasant so you will be able to answer everyone in the way you should.

COLOSSIANS 4:6

My children, we should love people not only with words and talk, but by our actions and true caring.

1 JOHN 3:18

PERSONAL NOTES TO THE GRADUATE | 119

COMMUNITY

"You must not hate your fellow citizen in your heart. If your neighbor does something wrong, tell him about it, or you will be partly to blame. Forget about the wrong things people do to you, and do not try to get even. Love your neighbor as you love yourself. I am the LORD."

LEVITICUS 19:17, 18

Let us think about each other and help each other to show love and do good deeds.

HEBREWS 10:24

We all have different gifts, each of which came because of the grace God gave us. The person who has the gift of prophecy should use that gift in agreement with the faith. Anyone who has the gift of serving should serve. Anyone who has the gift of teaching should teach. Whoever has the gift of encouraging others should encourage. Whoever has the gift of giving to others should give freely. Anyone who has the gift of being a leader should try hard when he leads. Whoever has the gift of showing mercy to others should do so with joy.

Your love must be real. Hate what is evil, and hold on to what is good. Love each other like brothers and sisters. Give each other more honor than you want for yourselves. Do not be lazy but work hard, serving the Lord with all your heart. Be joyful because you have hope. Be patient when trouble comes, and pray at all times. Share with God's people who need help. Bring strangers in need into your homes.

Wish good for those who harm you; wish them well and do not curse them. Be happy with those who are happy, and be sad with those who are sad. Live in peace with each other. Do not be proud, but make friends with those who seem unimportant. Do not think how smart you are.

If someone does wrong to you, do not pay him back by doing wrong to him. Try to do what everyone thinks is right. Do your best to live in peace with everyone. My friends, do not try to punish others when they wrong you, but wait for God to punish them with his anger.

ROMANS 12:6-19

EXCELLENCE

"So you must be perfect, just as your Father in heaven is perfect."

MATTHEW 5:48

Brothers and sisters, think about the things that are good and worthy of praise. Think about the things that are true and honorable and right and pure and beautiful and respected.

PHILIPPIANS 4:8

In all the work you are doing, work the best you can. Work as if you were doing it for the Lord, not for people.

COLOSSIANS 3:23

And now I will show you the best way of all . . . Love is patient and kind. Love is not jealous, it does not brag, and it is not proud. Love is not rude, is not selfish, and does not get upset with others. Love does not count up wrongs that have been done. Love is not happy with evil but is happy with the truth Love patiently accepts all things. It always trusts, always hopes, and always remains strong.

1 CORINTHIANS 12:31; 13:4-7

LOYALTY

"You must not speak against God or curse a leader of your people."

EXODUS 22:28

The LORD will keep all his promises;
he is loyal to all he has made.

PSALM 145:13

Whoever tries to live right and be loyal
finds life, success, and honor.

PROVERBS 21:21

A friend loves you all the time, and a brother helps in time of trouble.

PROVERBS 17:17

MORALITY

But there must be no sexual sin among you, or any kind of evil or greed. Those things are not right for God's holy people. Also, there must be no evil talk among you, and you must not speak foolishly or tell evil jokes. These things are not right for you. Instead, you should be giving thanks to God.

EPHESIANS 5:3, 4

Do not be fooled: "Bad friends will ruin good habits."

1 CORINTHIANS 15:33

Run away from the evil young people like to do. Try hard to live right and to have faith, love, and peace, together with those who trust in the Lord from pure hearts. Stay away from foolish and stupid arguments, because you know they grow into quarrels.

2 TIMOTHY 2:22, 23

Because you have these blessings, do your best to add these things to your lives: to your faith, add goodness; and to your goodness, add knowledge; and to your knowledge, add self-control; and to your self-control, add patience; and to your patience, add service for God; and to your service for God, add kindness for your brothers and sisters in Christ; and to this kindness, add love.

2 PETER 1:5-7

HONESTY

The honest person will live in safety, but the dishonest will be caught . . . The words of a good person give life, like a fountain of water, but the words of the wicked contain nothing but violence.

PROVERBS 10:9, 11

Good people will be guided by honesty;
dishonesty will destroy those who are not trustworthy.

PROVERBS 11:3

We show we are servants of God by our pure lives, our understanding, patience, and kindness, by the Holy Spirit, by true love, by speaking the truth, and by God's power. We use our right living to defend ourselves against everything. Some people honor us, but others blame us. Some people say evil things about us, but others say good things. Some people say we are liars, but we speak the truth. We are not known, but we are well known. We seem to be dying, but we continue to live. We are punished, but we are not killed. We have much sadness, but we are always rejoicing. We are poor, but we are making many people rich in faith. We have nothing, but really we have everything . . . You are not the same as those who do not believe. So do not join yourselves to them. Good and bad do not belong together. Light and darkness cannot share together.

2 CORINTHIANS 6:6-10, 14

You are God's child, and God will give you the blessing he promised, because you are his child.

GALATIANS 4:7

Your beauty should come from within you—the beauty of a gentle and quiet spirit that will never be destroyed and is very precious to God.

1 PETER 3:4

God chose you to be his people, so I urge you now to live the life to which God called you.

EPHESIANS 4:1

Every good action and every perfect gift is from God. These good gifts come down from the Creator of the sun, moon, and stars, who does not change like their shifting shadows. God decided to give us life through the word of truth so we might be the most important of all the things he made.

JAMES 1:17, 18

The will to live can get you through sickness, but no one can live with a broken spirit.

PROVERBS 18:14

PERSEVERANCE

My heart is steady, God;
my heart is steady.
I will sing and praise you.

PSALM 57:7

It is better to finish something
than to start it.
It is better to be patient
than to be proud.

ECCLESIASTES 7:8

Don't leave your job just because
your boss is angry with you.
Remaining calm solves great
problems.

ECCLESIASTES 10:4

Forgetting the past and straining
toward what is ahead, I keep trying
to reach the goal and get the prize
for which God called me through
Christ to the life above.

PHILIPPIANS 3:13, 14

God began doing a good work in
you, and I am sure he will continue
it until it is finished when Jesus
Christ comes again.

PHILIPPIANS 1:6

Let your patience show itself per-
fectly in what you do. Then you
will be perfect and complete and
will have everything you need.

JAMES 1:4

Smart people are patient;
they will be honored if they ignore
insults.

PROVERBS 19:11

Do not look out only for yourselves. Look out for the good of others also.

1 CORINTHIANS 10:24

We must not become tired of doing good. We will receive our harvest of eternal life at the right time if we do not give up. When we have the opportunity to help anyone, we should do it. But we should give special attention to those who are in the family of believers.

GALATIANS 6:9, 10

Jesus knew that the Father had given him power over everything and that he had come from God and was going back to God. So during the meal Jesus stood up and took off his outer clothing. Taking a towel, he wrapped it around his waist. Then he poured water into a bowl and began to wash the followers' feet, drying them with the towel that was wrapped around him . . . "If I, your Lord and Teacher, have washed your feet, you also should wash each other's feet."

JOHN 13:3-5, 14

"The Son of Man did not come to be served. He came to serve others and to give his life as a ransom for many people."

MATTHEW 20:28

"Whoever can be trusted with a little can also be trusted with a lot, and whoever is dishonest with a little is dishonest with a lot. If you cannot be trusted with worldly riches, then who will trust you with true riches? And if you cannot be trusted with things that belong to someone else, who will give you things of your own? "No servant can serve two masters. The servant will hate one master and love the other, or will follow one master and refuse to follow the other. You cannot serve both God and worldly riches."

LUKE 16:10-13

ABOUT THE AUTHOR

Laurie Beth Jones has written several national best–selling books, including *Jesus, CEO: Using Ancient Wisdom for Visionary Leadership*; *The Path: Creating Your Mission for Work and Life*; *Jesus in Blue Jeans*; *Jesus, Inc.*; and *Teach Your Team to Fish*. Her work has been featured in *Time, Business Week, CNN, Industry Week Magazine,* and *USA Today*.

After launching and running her own successful advertising agency for fifteen years, Laurie Beth Jones burst onto the national scene with *Jesus, CEO*, a book that espoused bringing spiritual principles back into the business world. That book, and subsequent books that followed, spent more than thirteen months on the *Business Week* Bestseller List, and have been translated into twelve foreign languages, with worldwide sales of one million copies.

Using practical wisdom, bursts of humor, and reality–based thinking, Jones has become one of the world's leading consultants for businesses that want to take their work—and their workers—to unparalleled levels of performance, satisfaction, and success.

Her work has reached as high as the White House, the Pentagon, the halls of Congress and the Senate, as well as the depths of workers in the streets of Calcutta, Bosnia, and South Africa. Her Path for Teens Program has received the blessing and support of Wal–Mart, and her Path Training Program is currently in use in the character development program at the United States Naval Academy in Annapolis, Maryland, as well as in various training programs around the country. She has been called upon by billionaires and kings, pastors, students, housewives, and prisoners to help discern their spiritual paths, and she lives out her mission daily, which is to "recognize, promote, and inspire the divine connection in myself and others."

For more information visit
www.lauriebethjones.com.

This is my prayer for you: that your love will grow more and more; that you will have knowledge and understanding with your love; that you will see the difference between good and bad and will choose the good; that you will be pure and without wrong for the coming of Christ; that you will do many good things with the help of Christ to bring glory and praise to God. PHILIPPIANS 1:9-11 NCV